RYA Pocket Guide to Boating Knots

Illustrations by Steve Lucas

© RYA 2006
First Published 2006
Reprinted August 2010, July 2011, April 2012, May 2013, June 2014, July 2015, May 2016, August 2017, June 2018, May 2019, November 2020, September 2021, July 2022, September 2023, August 2024, August 2025

The Royal Yachting Association
RYA House, Ensign Way, Hamble,
Southampton SO31 4YA

Tel: 02380 604 100

Web: www.rya.org.uk

We welcome feedback on our publications at publications@rya.org.uk

You can check content updates for RYA publications at www.rya.org.uk/go/bookschangelog

ISBN: 978-1-905104-72-7

RYA Order Code: G60

All rights reserved. No part of this publication may be reproduced, stored in a retrieval system, or transmitted, in any form or by any means, electronic, mechanical, photocopying, recording or otherwise, without the prior permission in writing of the publishers.

A CIP record of this book is available from the British Library.

Note: While all reasonable care has been taken in the preparation of this book, the publisher takes no responsibility for the use of the methods or products or contracts described in the book.

Cover Design: Creativebyte
Design: Creativebyte
Printed in the UK

1 Figure of Eight Knot

Useful as a stopper knot. To prevent a rope end running through a block, car, jammer, or dead eye. Easy to undo.

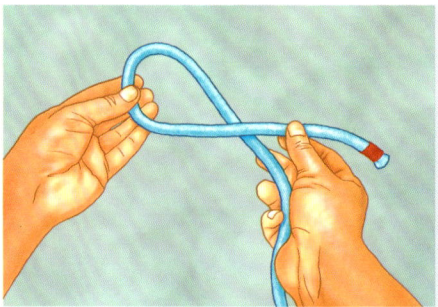

Make a loop.

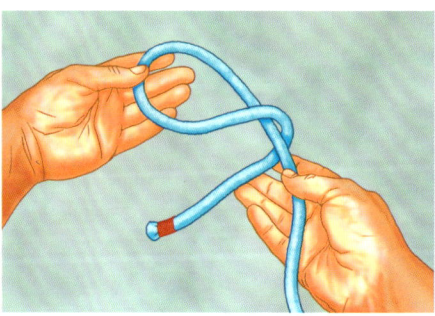

Pass working end under standing part.

- Before starting to tie a knot make sure the tail is long enough.
- When finished test the knot to make sure it is tight.

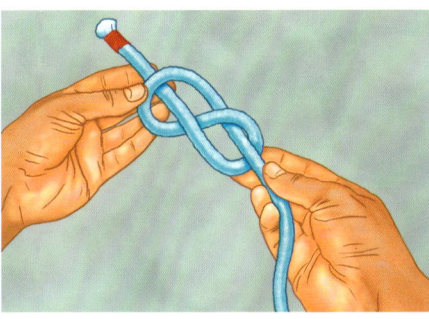

Pass working end down through the top loop...

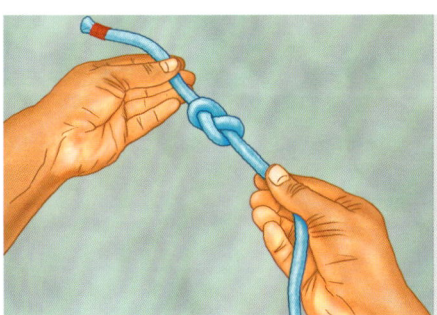

... and pull tight.

2 Clove Hitch

Useful for tying on fenders, attaching a rope to a post or lashing the tiller amidships. **Caution:** if not pulled tight at both ends, can work loose. Easy to undo.

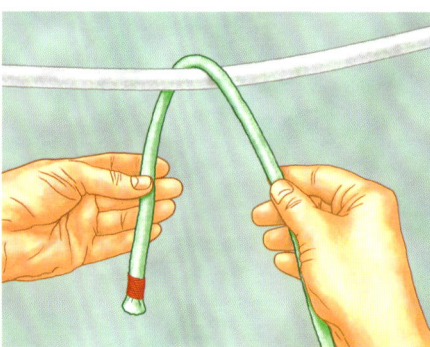

Pass working end around object, for example tiller/guardwire.

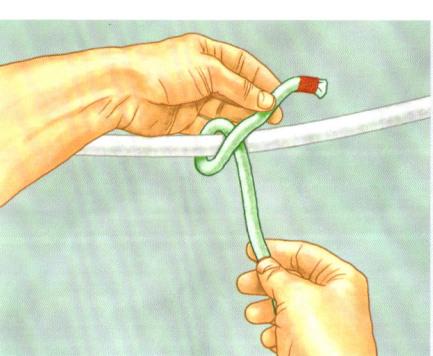

Pass working end back over again and then over standing part.

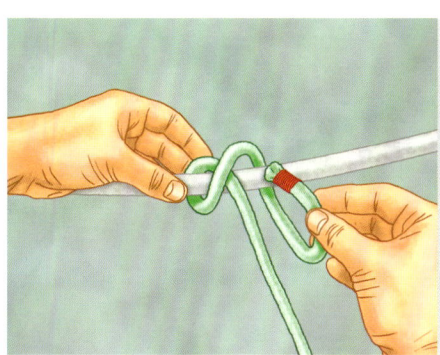

3 Pass working end around object again, then under standing part.

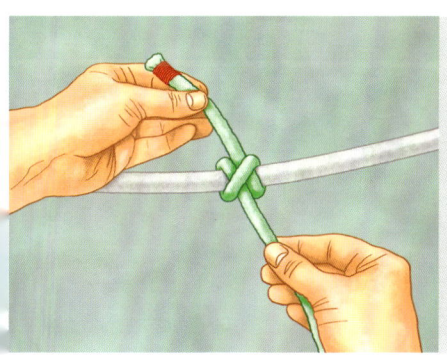

4 Pull tight.

3 Rolling Hitch

Used to temporarily relieve the strain on a working rope, when a sideways pull is required. This hitch will only grip when pulled in one direction and will slide when pulled in the other. Difficult to undo.

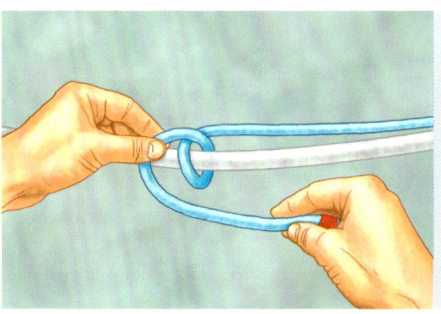

Pass the working end around the object/rope and then over the standing part.

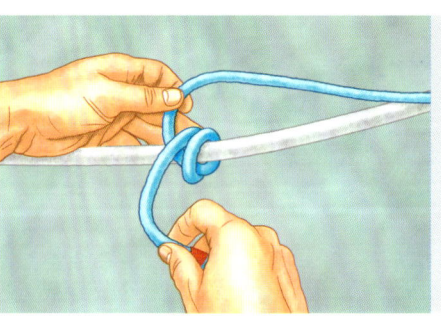

Pass the working end around the object/rope and over the standing part for a second time.

3 Pass the working end around the object/rope and under standing part. (Finish same as Clove Hitch then tighten).

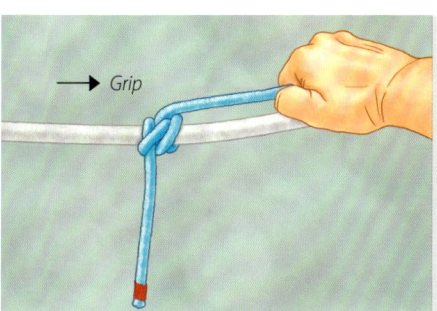

→ Grip

4 The knot will grip when pulled in this direction...

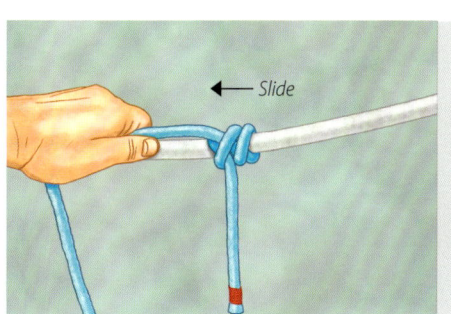

← Slide

5 ... and slides when pulled in the other direction.

4 Bowline

Used to make a secure loop in the end of a rope, for attaching jib sheets or to make a loop for mooring. Easy to undo.

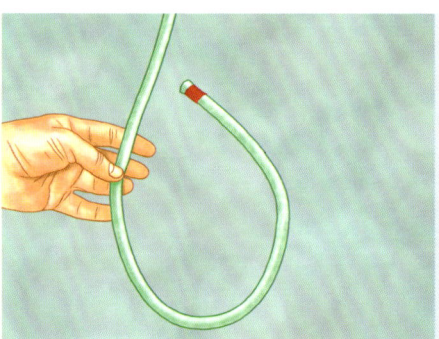

Make a small loop in the standing part.

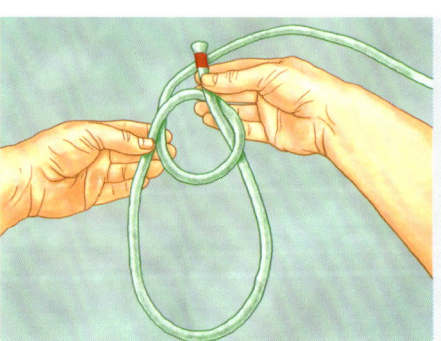

Pass working end up through the small loop.

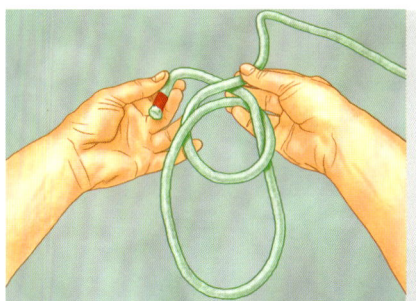

3
Pass working end under standing part.

4
Pass working end back down through small loop.

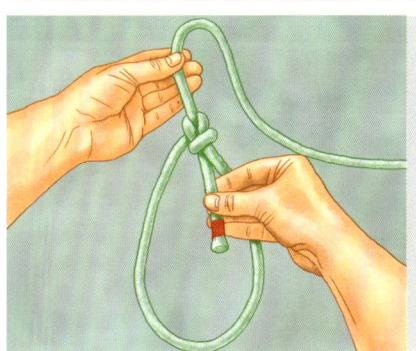

5
Pull tight.

5 Sheet Bend – Single

Used to join two ropes of similar thickness. A quick easy knot useful for joining two mooring lines/warps. **Caution:** when completed both rope ends should be on the same side of the knot. Easy to undo.

If there is a big difference in the thickness of the ropes or they are slippery use the Double Sheet Bend (page 12).

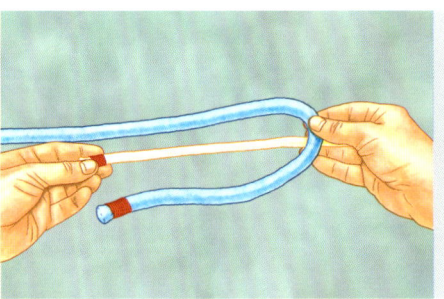

Make a bight in the thicker rope.

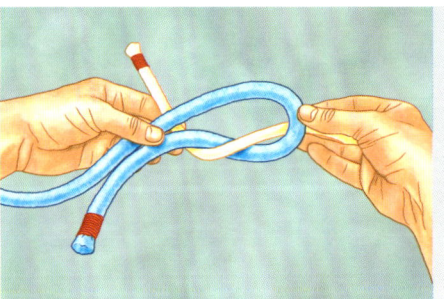

Pass working end up through and under the bight.

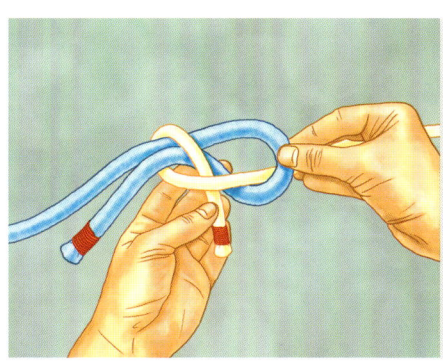

3 Pass working end over bight and under standing part.

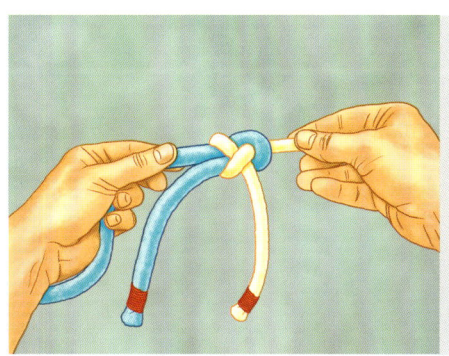

4 Check both ends are on the same side and pull tight.

6 Sheet Bend – Double

Used to tie a thin line to a very much thicker line or lines that are slippery. More secure than the Single Sheet Bend. **Caution:** when completed both rope ends should be on the same side of the knot. Easy to undo.

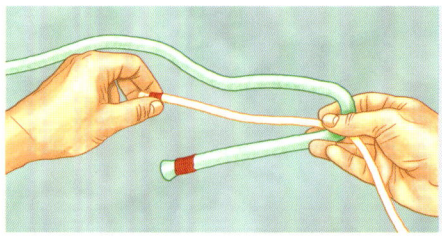

Form a bight in the thicker rope.

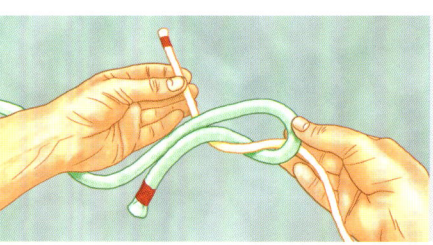

Pass the working end up through and under the bight.

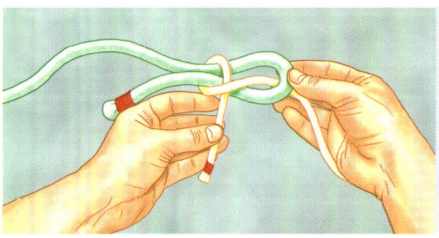

Pass working end over bight and under standing part.

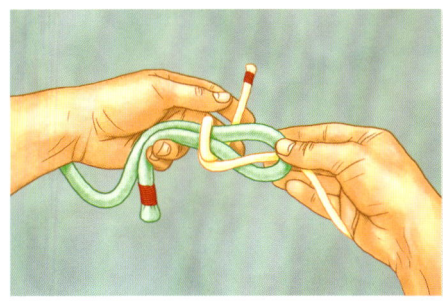

4
Pass working end under bight again.

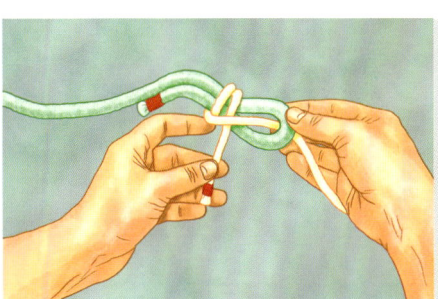

5
Pass working end over bight and under working part.

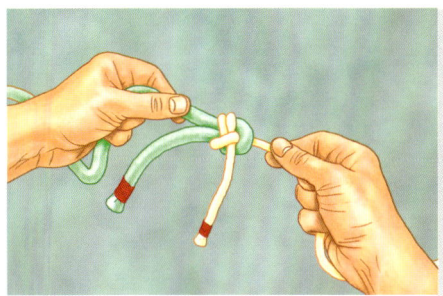

6
Check rope ends are on the same side and pull tight.

7 Reef Knot (or Square Knot)

Useful to tie in reefs to tidy sails, tying up or enclosing objects - sacks or bundles of sticks. **Caution:** the Reef Knot should never be used to join lines. Use a Sheet Bend. Easy to undo.

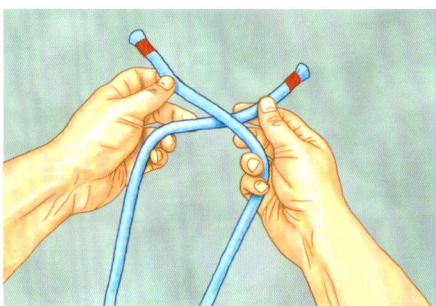

Pass the right working end over the left...

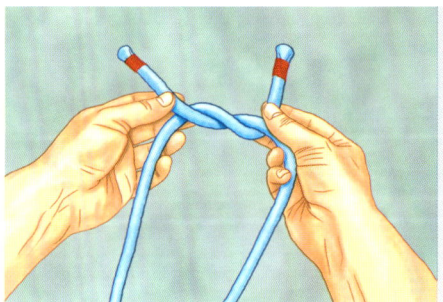

...and under.

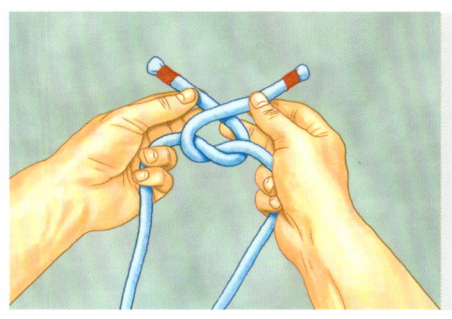

3 Pass the left working end over the right...

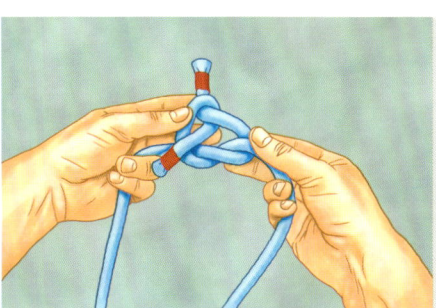

4 ... and under.

5 Pull tight on both ends.

8 Round Turn and Two Half Hitches

Useful for many applications such as securing a mooring line to a ring or for hanging fenders when coming alongside. A very versatile and secure knot. Easy to undo under pressure because holding the end keeps the tension on the Round Turn allowing you to undo the Half Hitches.

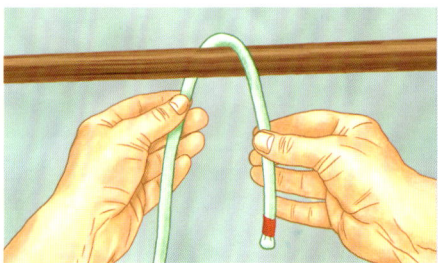

Pass the working end around the object.

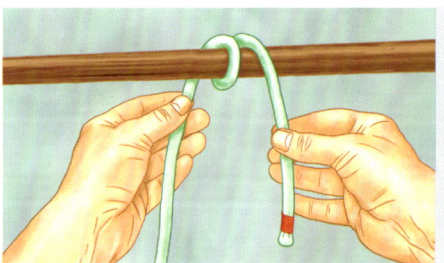

Pass the working end around again.

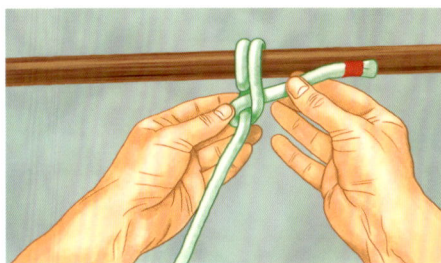

Pass the working end over and around the standing part.

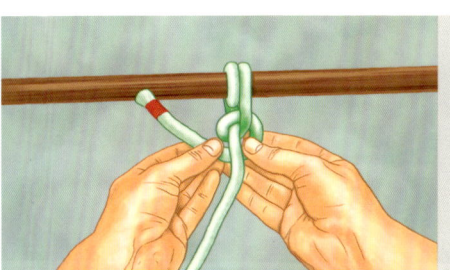

Pass working end over and around the standing part again.

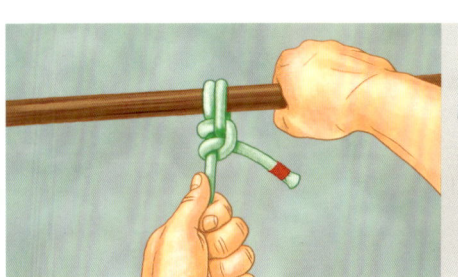

Pull tight.

Contents

1. Figure of Eight Knot — 2
2. Clove Hitch — 4
3. Rolling Hitch — 6
4. Bowline — 8
5. Sheet Bend – Single — 10
6. Sheet Bend – Double — 12
7. Reef Knot (for Square Knot) — 14
8. Round Turn and Two Half Hitches — 16

This simple little book contains all the really useful knots any boating person needs to know. The selection of these knots involved a long process of contacting lots of people and finding out what knots they actually used on their boats. Originally the idea was to have the favourite top ten, but following our research we discovered that there are really only eight knots that are regularly used by most sailors. So eight knots there are.

The book is compact enough to fit into your pocket and because of its design stays open, allowing you to use both hands to practise tying your knots. It is also waterproof so no excuses for not keeping one and practising on your boat.

RYA

RYA code G60

ISBN 978-1-905104-72-7